AWESOME ACCENT

DR JULIAN NORTHBROOK

CONTENTS

COMPLETE AUDIO VERSION OF
THE BOOK

The best learning happens by consuming the same information multiple times, and in multiple formats.

To help you with this, I've included a complete audio version of this book (as long as you have a smartphone that can use the "Learnistic" app).

Instructions for getting this can be found in the "Some Free Resources" section at the back of the book.

Important: the audiobook is only available via the Doing English Learnistic app, so if you don't have a smartphone this will be unavailable to you.

INTRODUCTION

How you sound in English matters. Research shows
this very clearly. Native speakers judge people with
clear, easy to understand accents as proficient in
English. *Even if in reality they're only beginners.* On the
other hand, they judge people whose accents are hard
to understand as being low-level. *Even if they're
"advanced" on paper.*

So I repeat: the way you sound in English matters.
Since you're reading this book, you probably know
this already. But here's the thing – sounding awesome
in English and having a clear, easy to understand
accent does **NOT** mean you have to sound like a Brit.
Or like an American. Or like anyone from the country
you live in or like what anyone else says you need to
sound like.

You see, the actual accent you speak with is nothing but a detail. And to be honest, a fairly minor detail at that. Yes, there are times when sounding like a native speaker of, say, British English, is better. But there are also times when speaking in your own accent is better. Sometimes other people receive you better if you're speaking with your own accent and not an English accent that's not "your own". I mean, personally, I find Eastern European accents sexy as hell. I'd far rather listen to that than say, the Geordie accent... which is a native British accent (but not one that I find particularly pleasant to the ear – sorry Geordies!).

The approach I take in this book is this: **you can speak with any accent you like, or indeed, accents, plural** (more on this later).

Your accent is a part of you. No matter what accent you speak in. And **that's** what's most important.

So we are going to talk about how you can learn a new accent. Whether it be a British one, an American one or whatever. But know that it's not necessary to chose an accent and a greater part of this book is going to be to focus on how you can improve your voice and the way you sound *regardless of what accent you speak with*.

Credit Where Credit's Due

Over the years I've had the opportunity to talk to some very intelligent—far more than me, I'm happy to say—people about accent and pronunciation. I've interviewed many language coaches and experts about all kinds of speech and communication-related topics – including accent. These interviews were for Doing English courses, and, of course, the *Extraordinary English Speakers* group (my group of superstar English learners).

This book is a combination of my own knowledge – most of which relates to the psychology of accents, how they work in the brain, but also the linguistics of accent—and also stuff I've learned from the people I've interviewed. Especially my good friend Jade Joddle, as well as Amy Walker of 21 Accents. See the **Resources Area** at the back where you'll find information about them.

What're We Going to Talk about in Awesome Accent?

In Chapter 1 I'm going to discuss all the background stuff you need. What is an accent, really? What does your accent say about you? How important is your accent when learning English as a second language? Do you need to live in a native-English speaking country? And a whole lot more.

In Chapter 2 we're going to discuss some mindset issues that are probably holding you back.

In Chapter 3 the three aspects of sounding awesome (only one of which is actually accent). Then, in Chapter 4—the main meat of this book—I'll share with you everything you need to know to learn any accent you want. How to do it, where to start, the most important things to know, and how to put changing your accent on autopilot so it just happens naturally and pretty much by itself over time.

Following this, the remaining chapters will go much, much deeper into various aspects of sounding natural and native-like when you speak, whether that's in a "native speaker" accent or in your own accent (hint: it doesn't make a difference if you do it right). Chapter 5 will look at the "lazy" sound – the most common (but often missed, ignored and unheard of) sound in English. Then in Chapter 6, we'll continue the discussion by looking at the way native speakers reduce, cut and 'chunk' their speech. Then in the final two chapters, we go waaaaay beyond mere accent and look at developing your voice to a high standard (again: regardless of what accent you choose to speak in).

I recommend you read at least chapters one to three in order, as these chapters provide the framework you need to improve your accent. After this, either read in order or pick and choose from the chapters that interest you most.

A Final Note

As with all of my books, *Awesome Accent* is not needlessly long. If you want a lot of pages for your money, this book isn't for you (go read a dictionary instead). However, if you want to learn to transform the way you sound in English quickly and effectively, read on.

I think of a good book as being like a woman's skirt – long enough to cover the essentials, but short enough to keep it exciting.

This said, there is also a certain amount of repetition. This is on purpose. Repetition aids learning, and the most important elements—the fundamentals—are repeated to make sure they stick.

With that, are you ready?

Let's get into the book and make some serious waves.

Best,

Dr Julian Northbrook

1
———

THE WHAT, WHY AND WHEN OF SOUNDING AWESOME

Accent is the way you sound. That much is pretty simple. But it goes much deeper than that. I mean, why do human beings even have accents? Why are there so many different accents? Why don't we all speak in exactly the same way? Surely it'd be a lot easier if we did?

Well, no, actually. It wouldn't. Accent plays an important role in our social systems. And it's worth taking a few minutes to discuss this because when you understand <u>why</u> something is the way it is, it's much easier to accept it and get good at it.

Really, what accent does is put you in a box. It's like a label that tells people who you are, where you're from and what class you're a part of. In a way it's your brand – a brand that makes you, boxes you and classifies you. You could even say that it's a "badge of identity".

The Badge of Identity

Yes. Accent is like a badge you wear to show you are part of a group. In that sense, it's similar to slang in that it makes you part of that group. The "in" group, as it were. Or, depending on your position, it'll also mark you an outsider, too (I guess you could say the "out-group").

When I was 19 I took a year off from studying at art school and bummed around London. I was between college and University and didn't really feel like going straight on to uni. So I went to London. Slept on sofas and occasionally in parks (seriously). Well, during that time I got to know some people who almost seemed to be speaking a totally different language to me. I remember a conversation that went something like this: *"Oi blad you wanna cotch at me manner like?"* Me: *"What?!"*

Yup, that was English.

Kinda.

And no, I wasn't sure at the time whether it was or not.

I mean, it sounded English... *kinda*. Only I didn't

have a clue what was being said to me. Turned out it was simple: *"Wanna hang out at mine?"* – I just wasn't used to the slang, the dialect or, indeed, the accent.

Different groups of people speak in different ways. And accent is, of course, an integral part of that. In terms of human evolution, these "in-groups" have always been very important. If you attended one of my *Small Talk Superhero* events, or indeed, took the Home Study Course (if you don't know what this is and are interested check my book *Advanced English Conversation*, available on Amazon Kindle, which is the precursor to Small Talk Superhero), you'll have heard me talk about this already. BUT – if you go back 100,000 years to the birth of the first human beings, and the beginning of language as we know it, you would have been totally reliant on your tribe for survival. The world was a wild, harsh place. People didn't survive long alone. And human beings, being what they are, it's not hard to imagine groups of fighting between each other, either. What this meant was that unknown people were dangerous. So we needed a system to maintain strong group bonds with the tribe (so that you were "known"). Well, that system was communication.

Small talk.

Conversation.

In-group speaking patterns.

Over time this would have evolved into what we see now – in-group slang, accents and speaking styles that people wear like a badge of identity.

So the question is, what badge are you wearing? Or, to put it another way, what box do you fit into?

What Box Do You Fit In?

So. Accent puts you in an in-group box.

It categorises you as being from a certain group of people. From a certain area. And a certain class. Generally speaking, accent is specific to the place you're from. A Japanese person speaks with a Japanese accent, a Chinese person with a Chinese accent, and so on. Obvious, I know. But then there are English accents, and these get a little confusing. Because we've got British accents, American accents, Canadian accents, Australian accents, Kiwi accents, Irish, Scottish, Welsh, and of course it goes down, down and down into micro-small area accents.

In the UK alone, for example, it is pretty easy to tell where someone is from based on their accent. This is likely true of most countries (it's certainly true of Japan). Whether the South, the North, from, say, Newcastle or even from what part of London.

England has 56 main accent types and within each one of those multiple sub-accents. So many, in fact, that nobody really knows exactly how many there are.

I grew up in the West-country and spoke (still speak) with a fairly general West-country accent. I never picked up an accent from any specific, small area because my dad liked to move around a lot. We lived in a different place almost every year until I started secondary school. That said, it was always around the West-country in general, so I did speak a pretty typical (and non-standard) dialect common to the West-country. More on that later.

Why Are There so Many British Accents?

So why are there so many accents?

Right off the bat – this is nothing unique to the UK, as I already alluded to. It's true of the US, Canada, Australia, New Zealand, and indeed every other country in the world, English speaking or not. But I only know the UK and England, so I'm going to use this as an example.

In fact, for simplicity, I'm just going to use England as an example. And also for simplicity, let's divide England up into four broad areas: The North, South, and the East and West Midlands.

Regional differences developed because of the historical way the English language itself developed. Up until the middle ages, people spoke a variety of different types of English. People in the North spoke "Northern" English, derived from Northumbrian Old English. People in the East and West Midlands spoke an English derived from Old Mercian English, and people in the South West an English derived from West Saxon. People in the East spoke an English derived from Kentish.

Then, over time, the area around London emerged as the power centre of England. And with it, the English spoken there became the most prestigious form of the language and, eventually, the standard.

I'm massively simplifying this of course. But over the centuries the different ways of speaking became gradually more and more like the standard, but each with their own distinct flavour. What's important for you, however, is to know that while yes, there is a "standard" British English—just like with any other country—the majority of people don't speak like that. Not exactly, anyway.

Language Constantly Changes

Again, this is the same anywhere, of course. But the way people sound and speak is constantly changing. On one hand, the varieties of English are becoming more similar.

Thanks to the internet and readily available media, what was once considered "English" or "American" has become blurred. Many idioms that were once British are now used in the US, and vice-versa – many Americanisms are now fairly standard on our side of the pond. I often use the term "to nail", meaning "to master" – which is listed in the Macmillan Dictionary as "mainly North American".

On the other hand, though, in a way, varieties of English are different, will always be different and are becoming more different. Think about people from your country: do they all speak the same? Of course they don't.

This creates a challenge for learning English (in general, but also its accents). What is the best type of English to model? Many people would say the "standard"—and in a sense, I agree—but the problem with that is that the vast majority of people don't speak the standard.

There's also the question of identity. People speak

like the people from their areas. And that means that just because you learn a standard British accent, that won't make you British per se.

Some researchers working on socio-linguistics (the relationship between language and social systems) say that it's a bad idea to speak English with someone else's accent.

If you're not American, so why sound American? Or, to put it another way, are you so ashamed of your own culture that you want to hide?

I will admit that I used to firmly believe this, though these days I take a much more relaxed attitude to the issue and say do whatever the hell you want.

A while ago I went to see a lecture here in Tokyo by an Australian researcher. It was about the relationship between language, identify and cultural assumptions.

One thing really caught my attention. It was a story about a guy who was having a lot of problems living and working in Australia. He was a Chinese guy. And he was a very high English level. This Chinese guy had spent a lot of time having accent training. And he sounded exactly like a British person with a flawless RP accent. Lots of people want this... but actually, THIS was the source of his problem.

People in Australia found him really uncomfortable to talk to. People thought he was weird, even. Here's this Chinese guy, in Australia, speaking with a posh British accent. There's this total lack of synergy between all these things. And anyway, it's not like he didn't make mistakes with his English – which also confused people, because initially, they thought he was British (we'll come back to this later).

You see, it's actually a very, very good thing if you speak with your own accent. If you are Chinese, and you have a Chinese accent, that identifies you as a Chinese person. It communicates a lot about who you are, where you come from, and your cultural identity and values. If you hide that accent you hide your identity.

Simply put, speaking with an accent that isn't your own is like wearing a mask. Or like when you talk to someone wearing sunglasses, and you can't see their eyes. It makes you hard to talk to. So what's the solution?

There isn't one.

Simple as that.

Ultimately, it all comes down to personal preference and what is going to make YOU happy. But the point is, it's not necessary to sound like a native speaker – so don't let anyone tell you it is.

The Key to Sounding Awesome

A lot of people are really concerned about their accents. And so logically their response to this is to try and *change* their accent. As we've already discussed, rather extensively, this isn't necessarily the wrong thing to do... but the <u>way</u> they do it is wrong. You see, instead of thinking about why their accent is a problem... they simply ask, *"How do I get an English accent?"* (or, American or whatever – you get the idea). But here's the truth: **for most people in most situations... <u>WHAT</u> accent you have doesn't make any difference at all.**

Yes, there are exceptions. There are always exceptions. But for most people, it's not about learning to sound like a Brit or like an American. Rather, *it's about working on the quality of your voice.* The way you express tone, emotion, rhythm and express yourself. While simultaneously working to improve your clarity.

And that's the key to sounding awesome.

Now, this doesn't mean you can't or shouldn't learn American or British Accents (or indeed, both). What it means is, first you've got to tackle the core problem. That you don't sound clear or easy to understand when you're speaking. That's what matters.

Making Your Accent Invisible

Actress, singer and "Accent Chameleon" Amy Walker told me that when she slips into an accent and gets it just right... *nobody notices*. The accent becomes totally invisible.

While it is cool and impressive to be able to do an accent well, unless you're showing off (and if you are, that's fine) you're using that accent because you want to be clear and easily understood.

Clarity.

And you don't necessarily have to sound <u>JUST LIKE</u> a person to be clear. The reality is, as we've already discussed, native speakers are used to hearing many different accents and ways of speaking. Take the average Londoner for example: London is a melting pot of languages and ways of speaking. Everywhere you turn people are speaking—and **SOUNDING**—different. So if people don't understand you well, it's not necessarily your accent that's the problem... otherwise, society would never function. London would be *doomed*. But what does matter —a lot—is that you're clear and easy to understand (have I said this enough times yet?)

And sounding clear and easy to understand... well, this gets quite complicated. Yes, your accent is a part of it. As is your pronunciation and intonation (we'll talk about those in Chapter 3). But it's also important that you chunk your English well (we'll talk about that in Chapters 5 and 6). And that you communicate the right feeling, tone and emotion when you speak (in the last couple of chapters). Simply put, there's more to it than just your "accent". But know this: **we all have a natural aversion to anything difficult.** And if you're difficult to understand... people will naturally want to avoid speaking with you. This is proven by science, by the way. This isn't just my opinion (it's all related to the whole in-group thing that we talked about).

When it comes to mastering a second language, there are so many things for us to learn and do and achieve. If you're going to truly nail a particular accent (and you don't have to go all the way – I'll talk about that later, too) you're going to need to put some serious time and effort into it. The method is simple, but that doesn't mean it's easy. But what I want you to get at this point is it's *all about clarity* – being easy to understand. And you've achieved your goal if people DON'T notice your accent (because that means you're doing something very, very right).

2

SOME SILLY MYTHS

B efore we go any further, there're a couple of frankly quite silly myths we need to clear up.

One of the biggest things that hold people back when learning English is their own limiting beliefs. If you think you can't do it – you won't be able to do it. Put simply, if your beliefs aren't in line with the result you want to get, you'll just get in your own way.

One such myth is the idea that you can't learn an accent as an adult.

It's Not Possible to Learn an Accent As an Adult

Can you master a new account as an adult if you grew up speaking a totally different language? Indeed, this is a contentious issue. But the answer is... *yes.*

Some people struggle more than others, I will admit. This is partly because some people pick up accents easier. Partly to do with where you come from – someone from, say, China is going to have a harder time than someone from, say, the Netherlands or Denmark (though they will also struggle with some of the sounds of English, it's just that there are less "alien" sounds for them to struggle with). And partly —and probably more importantly—because different people have very different standards and expectations regarding how they sound.

People who are very good at music do tend to just 'pick up' accents better than others. Of course, by 'pick up' we don't mean it just happens magically... that's bullshit. But if your ear is already trained to notice subtle differences in sounds, you're going to have a much easier time of it than other people. And if you're really good at singing, for example, and are used to monitoring your voice to make it sound right, then obviously this is going to make monitoring your own accent (which we talk about in Chapter 4) much easier.

This isn't talent of any such rubbish like that. It's simply a transferable skill. And there is scientific research to back this up. Researcher friends of mine have done some stuff on this – people who are very good at music find it much easier to learn the tone-based pronunciation of Chinese, for example. Personally, I'm useless at music... and when I studied Chinese, yes, I found the pronunciation extremely challenging.

I had a Japanese student here in Tokyo who started learning English in her late 40s and spoke with a beautiful, crisp British accent. Off the top of my head, I can think of at least 10 Extraordinary English Speakers members in various places around the world who speak with perfect "native speaker" accents. So yes, it can be done.

At this point though, I will say this: these people are at somewhat of a disadvantage. You see, if you speak with a foreign (i.e. non-English) accent any mistakes you make with your grammar or words go largely ignored. They're almost invisible because there's an expectation that you'll make mistakes. Remember what we said earlier? Accent is a badge of identity – a native speaker hears that you're not a native English speaker and expects you to make mistakes. The result is that the mistakes become invisible. Well, the problem my Japanese client (and everyone else in a similar boat) had was that her mistakes REALLY stood out. To the extent that people were confused. Initially, they thought she was a native English speaker... and so when she made a grammar mistake, they found it strange.

Anyway, I digress. The point is, it can be done. And many people do. You can too if you want.

Why You Might NOT Succeed

Motivation is a huge factor in whether you succeed or not.

Massive.

If you REALLY care about your accent, you'll take the pains necessary to perfect it. Simple. As. That.

This is what I meant before when I said differences in expectations and standards. Ultimately, if you don't really care that much... well, don't be surprised if you don't just pick up an accent, because you simply won't notice it. You won't be aware of your own imperfections, and you won't be aware of the way other people speak.

To be honest, this has always been my problem in

Japanese. My pronunciation and accent aren't bad... and I don't have any problem being understood, even though I do tend to get the accent wrong on some words (Japanese is a pitch based language). And when I'm getting lazy I let English-stress patterns creep in... and, yes, I know I do it. And yes, all being equal I'd like to fix it. But honestly? I simply don't care that much. And that's fine. If you don't care much either, that's fine too.

Several years ago I did some work with a voice trainer and cleaned up my Japanese accent a little, and one day I'll probably take it further. But for now? I've got better things to concentrate on, so whatever.

This is the same with any kind of English learning, of course, but it's going to require extensive experience and constantly hearing native pronunciation. Exposure. Input. And practice to get it right. And if you're not really motivated to completely perfect your accent? Well, again, you just won't (or at least, it's unlikely).

That said, if you're thinking of throwing this book away now – don't. Because although I will show you how to reach the levels of absolute perfection, it's not necessarily the approach I recommend for most people. Rather, I recommend taking an 80/20 approach and focusing on that all-important 20% the gives you 80% of the result.

Which is exactly what I did and still do – I'm learning Irish Gaelic right now, and very much taking an 80/20 approach. You can go a long way on that 80%. Then either ride on that and just worry about getting other shit done... or, if you REALLY do need to take it further than that, well, tackle that later.

I Need to Live in an English Speaking Country to Learn the Accent

Let's get this question out of the way now... 'cos it always comes up at some point. I hear this almost on a daily basis, and it makes no sense whatsoever if you just think about it.

Do you need to live in an English speaking country to learn its accent? No, no, and for fuck's sake, no.

This has got to be the biggest dumb, but very persistent myth about learning languages. That you're somehow at a disadvantage if you don't live in an English speaking country.

Honestly?

It doesn't make that much difference. And if you

use the techniques that we're going to talk about in this book then you don't need native speakers at all.

Practise is practise.

Using English is using English.

So what should you do instead? Simple: train your ear so you can become your OWN voice coach.

Here's an extreme, but illustrative example: The reason most (all that I know of, anyway) deaf people don't pronounce their speech, as well as people who can hear do, is, obviously, because they're deaf. They can't hear what they're saying. And so they can't adjust accordingly. Well, right now you're deaf too.

Or at least you are as far as your English pronunciation and accent are concerned. Because you're listening through the filter of your own first language. However, unlike the true deaf person, *you can learn to hear* – and that's what I'm gonna do here in this book. Teach you to hear, so you can sound how you want.

The only real advantage to living in an English speaking country as far as accent learning is concerned is that you're going to have a lot more voices to listen to. That is, more and varied exposure to how people speak. Great for building awareness of variation in accent and pronunciation. Perhaps not much of an advantage for developing your own, though. Ultimately you've still got to pick something and work with that. And you've still got to do all the awareness building work.

So honestly?

I'd argue that living in an English speaking country isn't an advantage at all. Not really. And I'm not the only one who thinks so. When I interviewed Amy Walker of 21 Accents, she told me that most of what she does is based on media she finds on the internet. Sometimes recordings she makes herself. And she told me she mastered the British Accent(s) before she ever went to the UK. Indeed, she also said this was an advantage. The problem with learning in the country, she says, is that it's emotionally very difficult to make the switch. People are used to you speaking like, well, you. If you then suddenly switch to say, an Australian accent, it's kinda surprising. Much easier is just to start in the accent you want to speak in right from the beginning... and that leaves you with no choice but to go at it alone, at least in the beginning.

Native Speakers Are Doing It Wrong!

This "myth" isn't really a myth.

'Cos it's kinda true.

Native speakers do say a lot of stuff "wrong". But

wrong isn't the same as "incorrect".

I'm forever getting comments on my YouTube videos saying that I pronounce such-and-such wrong, or I say such-and-such a thing wrong, blah blah blah. I'm not alone in this. I've had many a conversation with Jade about it. And I know from talking to other YouTubers that they all get the same thing. Well, here's the uncomfortable truth: **the English you learned at school ain't real English.** It's based on a "prescriptive" version of the language which is simplified and standardised and made all black-and-white.

In real English, there is no "correct" or "incorrect". No "right". No "wrong". No black or white. Only shades of grey.

Give Me a Chicken Soul!

In my book Think English, Speak English I talked about a silly mistake I made in Japanese.

I translated "Chicken Hearts" in my head (as in a type of skewered kebab that's common in Japan) and asked for "*tori no kokoro*" in a restaurant. The correct would have been *"hatsu"*, which means the chicken heart kebab (the food) I wanted to eat.

What I said would translate as "Chicken Soul", which, for ages, my wife laughed at me about it – to the extent where if I ever laughed at her English she came back with, "TORI NO KOKORO!". But then after publishing TESE, something funny happened: One reader emailed me to say that actually, in Kansai (a part of Japan), people DO call this particular delicacy *tori no kokoro* – something which Mrs Northbrook didn't know. So although she kept laughing at me because it was wrong, actually, technically, it was right. Just the wrong part of the country (she no longer uses this as a way to take the piss out of me).

The point is if something seems wrong to you... it might be. But it might not be. So keep an open mind.

Japanese Pitch Accent Woes

One final, very quick example here, directly related to accent and voice. Again, it's from Japanese.

Japanese uses a *pitch based* accent, and some words change in meaning depending on where you put that accent. So if you say, "HAshi", with the pitch on "ha", that means chopsticks. But if you say, "haSHI" with the accent on "shi", that means bridge.

Simple in principle, tricky in execution. And what makes it really tricky is that there is little consistency between areas of Japan. Different people put the pitch in different places. So it'd be easy for me, the

Japanese learner, to learn the standard Tokyo pitch accents... then get frustrated with people from other areas who're doing it "wrong". Only they're not doing it wrong. Just differently.

Take the word "arigatou" as a simple example, meaning "thank you". People in Tokyo say, "aRIgatou", people in Osaka say, "ariGAtou", and people in Nagoya say, "arigaTOu".

Which is right? Well, the Tokyo accent is the standard, so I guess the Tokyo accent. But that in no way makes the other accents incorrect.

The point is when it comes to language (especially English) variation is the rule, not the exception. So when you're going through the process I teach here, put your own opinions and expectations to one side for now. Be flexible. Experiment. And learn instead of arguing.

3

THE THREE ASPECTS OF SOUNDING AWESOME

R ight, let's start with the basics of the basics. What even is an accent? I know we've already talked about what an accent is in terms of the "socio-linguistic" side (everything we talked about in Chapter 1) – but how do we actually define an accent. The thing you're gonna learn?

On the surface, at least, accent is simply the way you sound. That is kinda obvious, I know. But many people do misunderstand what accent really is. You see, accent should (though often isn't) be thought of as separate from pronunciation and from intonation (and of course these contain all kinds of other subcategories, too – tone, rhythm, and so on).

For now though, let's just focus on these three

main components – Accent, Pronunciation and Intonation.

Accent, pronunciation and intonation are not the same thing. And although, yes, you'll likely learn them together... you should think of them as being separate. Take pronunciation, for example – this is not the same as "accent".

Perfect Pronunciation?

The word "pronunciation" is a technical word for talking about how particular sounds are said in speech. Accent is how you sound when you say it... but pronunciation is how it is supposed to be said.

In a sense, getting the pronunciation right is far more important than what accent you speak with. Because, obviously, if you're not pronouncing words right you may be misunderstood.

Pronunciation is also the easiest part of sounding awesome to learn. It's pretty black and white – you either pronounce word right, or you don't. Yes, there is variation between different countries or dialects of English. But it's far more consistent than accent, which changes from person to person.

The Difference Between Pronunciation and Accent

For a really easy to understand example of this, lets once again look at the Japanese language.

Japanese follows a very regular consonant-vowel pattern. Most words (unless they end with an "n" sound) end with a vowel sound. For example, the Japanese word for "eat" is "taberu", and the past form is "tabeta".

See how that works?

Consonant-Vowel—Consonant-Vowel.

Ta-be-ru.

The result of this pronunciation-pattern is that Japanese people often put vowels onto the end of English words where they shouldn't be. For example: *"I donto thinku that isu righto"* – see what I mean?

This was always a huge source or frustration for me (and students) when I was a secondary school teacher. Because to my students, speaking with correct pronunciation and ending words on consonants would feel very strange. And without me constantly pushing them, they'd naturally fall back into the Japanese consonant—vowel pattern of speaking. Importantly here, though, **this is a problem of pronunciation *not* accent.** Even if I say *"I donto thinku* *that isu righto"* in my typical British accent, *it still sounds strange.*

On the other hand, a Japanese person may speak with perfect pronunciation ("I don't think that is right") but still speak with a Japanese accent. See how that works

Adding Intonation to the Mix

There's another problem Japanese people commonly have to do with 'intonation'. Intonation is what is really important in terms of nailing the 'musicality' of your speech (and it's something we're going to talk about a lot later in the book in terms of rhythm, tone and expression in speech).

The musicality of your speech is what makes you an engaging speaker. And it's what makes you easy to understand if you use it well.

Intonation is important.

Japanese people—and Asian people in general, though of course people from other countries too often also find this hard, as I said. Japanese is pronounced in a very flat regular manner without stress. Japanese follows a very regular beat.

Ta-be-ru.

Each syllable has the same amount of time allocated to it – it's very regular. This means that Japanese people tend to speak English in quite a flat, regular way because they apply this same regularity to English. This is a problem because to native English speakers this sounds very monotonous and we lose a sense of what is important and what isn't in your speech (we'll talk about this in detail in Chapter 8).

Personally, I find the opposite hard in Japanese. I tend to put rhythm and stress into my speaking that shouldn't be there. And have to concentrate to tighten up my speaking. For example. I might say something like "konnichiwa" (hello) as "KonnnniiiCHIwa", extending and stressing sounds – which sounds very unnatural in Japanese (but is very common among western people speaking Japanese as a second language).

In a nutshell, intonation is closely related to accent. But it's not the same. It's still separate in that you can still have perfect intonation but speak with your own original accent. And likewise, you can have a perfect British accent (for example) and still speak with un-nativelike intonation. Again, we'll talk about this in detail in Chapters 7 and 8.

HOW TO NAIL ANY ACCENT YOU WANT: THE QUICK 'N' DIRTY GUIDE

Right. Enough waffle. Let's get into the nitty-gritty how-to of this. This chapter is the main meat of Awesome Accent. The other chapters are important (especially the last two, which take you well beyond mere-accent) but if you just wanted to learn how to learn an accent, quick 'n' dirty, you could get by with just reading this chapter.

Step 1 - The First Step

The first step to nailing an accent isn't what most people expect. Hell, it's not what I expected either. But when I interviewed Amy Walker about how she learns so many accents wicked fast, this was the advice she gave me.

The first step is to really want to learn an accent. Plain and simple.

You might think this is kinda silly... you're reading a book about learning an English accent. How could you NOT want to learn an English accent?

Thing is though, people often don't actually know what they want. They want to sound better in English. That's for sure. But they're actually not sure why they sound so shit now. This is why I've included two chapters at the end of this book that go waaaaaay beyond accent.

Do you really want to give it a strong focus for years to get to that level? What would be the benefit to you? Do you really think that you couldn't be promoted at work or you couldn't do certain things because of your accent not being 100% native?

I don't think so.

Though, of course, I guess it does depend on the job and a whole load of other things.

Ultimately, for people learning English, your accent is a little bit like masturbation. It's fun for you, and we all wanna do it (even if you don't admit it) but it's also selfish and only for ourselves. We come up with lots of reasons, but really we learn specific accents because we want to fit in, or simply because we love doing it. Because all the "logical" reasons for learning an accent don't make sense. Not sounding like a Brit isn't making you hard to understand. Your bad pronunciation or inability to express yourself well might be. But that's not accent.

But you know what?

There's nothing wrong with a bit of masturbation.

And if you want to learn that accent 'cos you think it sounds cool, great. Do it. But if you're going learn an accent and put the time and effort required into mastering it – you'd better love it.

Fascination

Amy Walker says you've got to be fascinated by your chosen accent, and I agree. In fact, this goes for anything we do. Life's too short for messing around with things we don't want to do.

Honestly?

For most jobs and people in most circumstances, it's not important or necessary to speak with a specific accent. Your OWN is perfectly good enough. And again, sometimes even preferable (with the rule that you must be clear).

Jade told me that she works with people from all over the world in senior, high-level management positions. People who go right to the top. Never once has not being able to speak with a certain accent been a barrier.

This has been my experience too. But here's where accent IS important – it's all about how you FEEL. And if you don't FEEL good speaking English then you will make it a barrier.

Say, for example, you're taking a job interview. If you're all, "Oh my god, I'm so embarrassed about my accent..." you won't perform your best. You're not going to be confident, and you're probably not going to get the job.

So the short answer is that yes. You should take the time to work on your accent alongside the rest of your English. Whether that's learning to speak like a Brit, an American or simply with your own native accent. Which doesn't matter – what matters is that you're clear and HAPPY with the result.

If you feel better speaking like the queen? Or you want to sound like Donald Trump? Do it.

Step 2 - The Big N

There was a house on the street corner near where I used to live. I walked past that house every day for years. Then one day it was gone. I went away for the weekend, and when I walked past on Monday morning, the corner was just a patch of bare ground. The house had totally vanished.

This isn't unusual in Tokyo. Houses go up and come down fast. They're made of wood, and it doesn't take much to knock them down.

The strange thing is though...*no matter how hard I think now, I have no idea what that house looked like.*

What colour were the walls? What kind of door did it have? What shape was the roof?

I walked past it every day, multiple times for years, but I can't remember.

Why?

Because I never actually paid attention to that house. It was there, in the background. But I never really *noticed* it. Not until it was gone, anyway.

Why You Don't "Pick Up" Accents

When it comes to learning an English accent (or indeed anything to do with English) you'll never learn what you don't notice. If you say something wrong, but don't know you say it wrong, you'll never fix it.

A good example of this is my own pronunciation.

In certain areas of the UK people pronounce the "TH" sound like an "F" or a "V" (depending on where in the word it is) – something called "th-fronting". Many people consider it a lazy, uneducated accent (and it is in a way) but it's also pretty widespread. Th-fronting is a prominent feature of Cockney (which is probably where it's most known). Also the Essex dialect, Estuary English, some West Country (which is where I'm from – I grew up speaking a dialect common in North Devon) and Yorkshire dialects, Newfoundland English, African American Vernacular English, and Liberian English.

I grew up speaking like this and said "fink" instead of "think", "brover" instead of "brother" and so on.

The point is, I grew up with this. And I didn't get interested in languages or dialects until after I started teaching – so I never actually realised I said it wrong. When I was a kid, everybody around me spoke like that. When I was older, I simply didn't notice (the "TH" sound simply wasn't a part of my pronunciation set). It's kinda embarrassing to admit now, but I actually thought (fought haha) that "TH" was just an alternative spelling for "f". It wasn't until I started teaching English and someone asked me about it that I even realised I pronounced it wrong (technically I didn't pronounce it "wrong" – I spoke with a dialect).

The funny thing is though, once I noticed it, it was like a big set of floodgates opened. I started to notice the "th" sound EVERYWHERE, and I became hyper-aware of how I said it.

The thing is, I never really cared (and still don't).

It's one way of speaking among many. So I didn't try to "fix" it.

Then later, when my kids went to an Indian international school in Tokyo and we got to know a lot of people who spoke with Indian dialects. And I started to notice the sound even more.

Indian accents tend to pronounce "TH" as "T" – so "eart" instead of "earth", "tink" instead of "think", and so on. And of course, my kids wanted to know why. So I explained... and again, because I became hyper-aware of the "TH" sound, I started to hear it everywhere.

And somewhere along the line... I decided I would change the way I pronounced it (doing exactly what I'll talk about in a moment).

As a result, my pronunciation started to change – really, without me even thinking about it. Once I was aware, and once I made the decision to change it... it just changed. Yes, it took a little time. And yes, for a while I got it wrong sometimes. But now I use the standard "TH" completely normally and find speaking with an "f" instead of a "TH" strange.

Again, it's all about noticing.

Or, to put it another way – awareness.

So what are some good ways to build awareness of

sounds that you might be getting wrong, or that are different from what you're used to?

Glad you asked...

Where to Start?

As a language learner, you might be listening out for words that you don't know in a sentence. Or listening for words that you do know. "Oh, I know what they're saying." I know you might be concentrating on the actual vocabulary. But what I'm telling you to do is to switch that focus and start to think about the sounds, actual sounds of speech. And that's really what awareness training is.

Opinion differs on this, but if you work with a coach they may point out the mistakes you make. That is, the sounds you produce that are different to what you want to produce.

And this is valuable.

Sure, it is.

BUT – and this is a big "but", just because someone's pointed it out, that doesn't necessarily mean you're going to pay attention or notice it. Especially if they're pointing out all kinds of different errors and you get overwhelmed.

Personally, I prefer to push people to notice these things themselves, first.

When I tell you that you do something, you may

pay attention. But probably not. But when you come to a conclusion yourself? That's much, much more powerful.

When I notched the "TH" sound, nobody told me, "you do it wrong" as such. Rather, I became aware of the sound when someone asked me about it and I noticed myself that I was using a non-standard dialect. Nobody "fixed" my mistake. Nobody even said I made a mistake. It was simply a question asked out of curiosity. And because I noticed it, I became aware of it. And over time I decided to change it in exactly the way I'll describe in the next section.

But first, start by looking up the common pronunciation problems for people with your first language.

Multicultural London English

Since we're already talked about th-fronting, let's talk about a similar example.

Multicultural London English.

This is a kind of street language that is common in the UK. One of the features of this accent is that "T" is often replaced by "D". So someone would say, "Oh, dat man." Or, "have you seen dis?"

When you hear that, of course, you understand what they're saying – "that" man, or have you seen "this"?

Let's say someone who speaks like this every day

wanted to change their accent. They want to learn a more standard English accent.

Would they want to do that?

Dunno.

Who cares – this is just an example.

But what they would start by doing is identifying the sounds that they habitually make that are different to the target (standard) accent. Which we've done – "T" is said like a "D".

Then they would start looking out for that sound in the speech of others, but more importantly in their OWN speech.

Think of this like a program running constantly in your mind. Not at the forefront of your mind, but somewhere near the surface. You're not thinking about it all the time, but it's there. Humming along in the background.

So you're talking. Having a conversation with someone. Talking, talking, and THERE – you say it: "Oh, have you seen dat?"

Make a mental note of it – say to yourself, "that's the sound I'm looking for."

And that's it.

As soon as you catch yourself saying it, just make a mental note of it. No need to correct yourself out loud. Just do it silently in your head: "Have you seen that?"

Make sense?

Good.

You spot yourself doing it, and then you correct it. In your head.

It's not like you have to point it out to anyone.

You just want to capture it.

Slowly, over time, start replacing the sound with the new sound – start saying, "T" instead of "D".

Now, don't expect that because you know it you'll be able to say it in the new (correct) way 100% of the time. You won't. That's not how the brain works. Most of it's running on autopilot, and while that's a good thing, sometimes it's gonna autopilot right over the stuff you want to change.

That's fine.

Don't stress about it.

Just give it time.

As an English learner, this is actually easier for you. So in a way you're lucky. But if you're a native speaker, you've got a lifetime habit of saying it in a different way. So have realistic expectations for yourself. When I started changing my "TH" pronunciation, there was a period where my pronunciation was erratic. I'd get it right sometimes, wrong others. But that's fine. It's all part of the process. Try to just keep one sound at the forefront of your awareness, just below the surface. It can take around three months for that sound to completely shift (which is about how long it took me to nail the "TH" sound). And you're not going to do it 100% of the time. Just aim to get it right 80% of the time. Then once you've got that, move on to a new sound.

It's completely normal to slip backwards and forwards, too. Some days you'll get the accent spot on.

Others you won't.

As you can see, perfecting a single sound can take some. For a native speaker changing a single sound, this isn't a problem. But for you, you probably have multiple sounds you need to change. So we need to start with the most important sounds – the "big wins", which we'll talk about in a moment.

But first, a quick warning...

Be Careful of over Correction

When you start to change a sound, in the beginning, you'll go too far with it and start overcorrecting.

So in the example above, you'll start fixing the "D" pronunciation and start saying, "that" instead of "dat", but you'll also likely that saying things like, "tart" when you wanted to say, "dart".

This was something I had a problem with when I

started to become aware of my own "f" accent (where it should have been "TH") when I was teaching in schools and wanted to teach with a more standard pronunciation. I'd find myself lisping things and saying, for example, "thind" instead of "find".

It's like the program running just below consciousness went into overdrive and started to replace ALL the "f" sounds with "TH" – not really surprising, when you think about it because for a long time those sounds were the same to me. Once again awareness is key.

Notice you're doing it, and it'll stop itself. Now, on to those all-important "Big Wins".

Step 3 - Get Yourself Some Big Wins

Once you've got an idea of what the major problem areas are, you need to start fixing them.

With enough awareness, this will start to fix itself (but you've got to consciously and objectively listen to other people and yourself). But we can speed the process up by focusing on the most important stuff and TRYING to fix them.

Let's use Japanese English as an example since it's one that I know a lot about. First, ask yourself what the main sounds that people from your country (in this case Japan) have. You probably know most of these anyway, or are aware of them on at least some level. If you're not sure, google is your friend. These are going to be your big wins.

Lip My Tights!

Every country has its own stereotypical way of speaking English.

This point very nicely exemplified in the film "Lost in Translation". There's a scene where Bob Harris is in his hotel room when someone knocks on the door. It turns out to be, of all things, a call girl that someone's sent up for him. But not just any call girl. Ohhhh no. This is a rape fantasy call girl. And she wants him to rip her stockings. Or at least, that's what she means anyway... because what she actually says is, "Lip my stockings! Lip them!" Bob looks confused before getting the idea (and soon after asks her to leave).

Doing It 80/20 Style

Now, I'm not sure if rape fantasy call girls exist in Japan (I'm sure they do – and not just in Japan). But the point is, it's kind of a stereotype that Japanese people can't do a proper English "R". Japanese has a single sound that is something like a mix of "R" and "L" (much closer to "L" though).

If you're Japanese, you already know this. And you

should also know that it's a great thing to start with. Because just eliminating these obvious, stereotypical sounds is going to have a disproportionate effect on how clear you sound. It's 80/20 at it's best – 80% of the result for just 20% of the effort.

So, get on Wikipedia and Google and start looking stuff up.

Here's an Example...

Right now I'm interested in Irish English.

A quick google search tells me that in the Irish accent it's very common for "I" sounds to be pronounced more like an "oi" sound – "oirish", "oire-land". It's not quite "oi", though, because if you listen very carefully that "o" has a bit of an "a" sound in there too. It's basically impossible to write this. But you get the idea.

The "TH" sound is also often removed and comes out more like a "T" or a "D" (not dissimilar from Indian English") – "tink" or "dis"; "What do you tink of dis"

Irish speakers also tend to pronounce the "r" in words. In British English, we'd say "park" without an "R" sound (more like "pahk") – but in Irish English

English that "r" would be pronounced. So it'd be more like, "PaRk".

Another common feature of Irish English is that the "L" sound pronounced in the back of the mouth in British English (for example in, "bottle") is pronounced at the front of the mouth in Irish English. Just like the "L" in, say, "lovely".

Finding this information took me about 10 minutes. Of course, this isn't even close to covering all the features of the Irish English accent, they are some of the big "80/20" sounds. This means that if I JUST got good at these... I'd be doing pretty damn well.

Now, as I talked about above, I wouldn't want to try and get good at these all at once. It'd be too much. Overwhelm is a bad thing and it leads to getting nothing right. Instead, what I'd want to do is pick a single sound and listen out for this as much as I can. Practise saying it. Moving my mouth. Moving my tongue. Again, the most important thing though is awareness. Really NOTICING that the sounds exist, and how they differ from what I'm used to.

Step 4 - Build Motor Skills

So you find your specific problem. Build awareness by noticing it in other people's English and your own.

And you train the muscles to do what they're supposed to do.

This can be hard.

Which is why you really want to be focusing on those "big" sounds first and foremost.

Also, don't worry if you can't do it well immediately. Actively practising sounds should be combined with listening out for the sounds in other people. That is, awareness. You need to be constantly learning about the sound and adjusting your own pronunciation as you go. Work out the tongue placement and how your mouth should move. Watch people and the way they say things. Notice how their mouth muscles move, right up their face, in their cheeks and even around the eyes.

Again, don't worry if it takes time to get it right. Given time you'll naturally fall into the right way of putting your tongue in the right place and slowly make the right sound.

A Motor Awareness Exercise

Now, you can greatly speed this process up.

How?

By building awareness of your own mouth, that's how.

We'll talk about this in a lot more detail in Chapter 7 when I talk about some exercises for building expression in your voice. But one good way to improve fast is to get a mirror and practise purposely screwing up.

Play around with the sound.

Purposely do it wrong.

Mess it up and try and make yourself laugh. Now try doing it right. Listen carefully to the difference, and also watch how your mouth and facial muscles move. Now watch a native speaker saying the sound. How does it compare to your own?

Keep practising and adjusting.

Again, don't worry if it doesn't come right away. It doesn't matter. Have fun with it, and just notice how your mouth works.

Manipulate your face, mouth and lips and try to make all kinds of different sounds. Become intimately familiar with your own mouth and face.

When you do this, by the way, you'll find you get quite tired. Your tongue is weak like a baby's. It's like lifting weights in the gym. Your mouth, tongue, lips and face are used to moving in certain ways. And if you start forcing them to move in new ways, well, they're having to grow and adapt.

It's going to a new place where it doesn't know how to go yet.

So it feels a bit weird when you put your tongue

there because you have never done it... and so your natural reaction is to NOT do it.

Getting Past the Weird

In Chapter 3 I talked about the problem many beginner Japanese learners have. Adding vowel sounds to wordsu thato shouldn'to havu themu.

Well, when I was a secondary school teacher (especially at a private girl's school I used to teach at) one of the big problems I have was with students feeling weird about correct pronunciation. Yes, they were embarrassed to say it correctly. What can I say? Teenagers are weird. But, you see, it was because it wasn't familiar to them. And as a result, it was uncomfortable. And therefore they felt embarrassed – more so than pronouncing it wrong.

To get those sounds that don't exist in your language, often that requires sort of like tongue physiotherapy. That's going to be the most challenging aspect of you learning a sound because it's a new position.

By way of analogy, when I first came to Japan I wasn't that good with chopsticks. But there was NO WAY I was going to eat with a spoon while everybody else used them... so I persevered.

You know how long it took for the base of my hand to stop cramping up every time I ate dinner?

Around four years.

No joke.

The little muscles in my hand that are engaged when using chopsticks were never used before. The result was that they had to be trained and toughen up.

Before We Move On...

Really, that's it.

Not what you don't know. Learn how to do it, train yourself with practise. I'm not going to talk about specific exercises for building motor skills in this chapter because I cover them in detail in Chapters 7 and 8.

But again, the key to the whole thing is noticing.

Building awareness. And constantly, iteratively improving your pronunciation and accent over time. If you do your research well, you'll know exactly what sounds are important in the accent you're learning. And if you're spotting those sounds in other people and in your own speaking, this will take you a long way and the rest becomes pretty simple. The key really is awareness. It sounds too easy, I know. But it is as simple as that.

5

THE LAZIEST SOUND IN ALL OF HUMAN SPEECH

Why do native speakers seem to speak so fast? A lot of people believe native speakers speak really fast. They don't. Not really.

Rather, it's just that people don't know the sounds they're hearing... and as a result, their brain can't keep up. Another reason is to do with the way we crush down our language. This is a very important feature of "chunks", something I know a lot about (probably more than the majority of the people in the world) and will talk about here (but for detail I'm referring you to Master English *FAST*).

In this chapter and the next, we're going to look at two very important aspects of this. The "schwa" sound in this chapter, and then in Chapter 6 "Elision".

The Schwa? What's That When It's at Home?

Want to speak smoothly in English?

Of course you do.

That's why you're here, after all.

Well, here's a secret – there's one very, very important sound in English that getting right will have a MASSIVE effect on your English. It's not even 80/20. More like 99/1.

Something called the Schwa.

Never heard of it?

Don't worry, most people haven't.

The word itself doesn't sound very English, and originally it wasn't. It actually comes from Hebrew. In Hebrew writing, "shva" is a vowel diacritic (a little thing that drops down below letters) that indicates an 'eh' sound (which is not the same as our schwa). The term was then adopted by German linguistics in the 19th century Germany philologists. Which is why we use the German spelling, "schwa."

Most—probably all—languages have the schwa sound, and any vowel can become a schwa.

But this still doesn't tell us what it is.

The schwa has been called the murmur vowel, the indeterminate vowel, the neutral vowel, the obscure vowel, and the natural vowel. And the thing that links all these names is the fact the schwa is under pronounced and almost invisible.

The schwa is actually the most common sound in the whole of the English language. Which might be surprising considering, again, most people have never heard of it. And it's not even represented in the standard alphabet. Though you'll often see it in dictionaries and phonetical spelling represented as a "ə"— an upside-down e).

Yep, it's everywhere.

Big words.

Little words.

Absolutely bloody everywhere. Native English speakers are constantly making the sound of schwa.

What Kind of Words Uses This Sound?

The words "a" and "the" are the most common words in English.

Yet, they are notoriously difficult to learn.

Why is this?

Because we don't really pronounce them, that's why. They are very much understated and 'soft' in naturally flowing speech. That is, they tend to be "schwaised" (unless we're emphasising something – more on that in a moment).

One reason so many people struggle with these tricky little words is that they don't get the schwa.

If you think about kids learning to read, the way they read is quite unnatural. They read word by word, one word at a time. And they fully pronounce words like "the" and "a" – which isn't how we say them in speech at all. Which is why kids' reading doesn't flow well.

In speech, these words are schawised. They're unstressed and under-pronounced.

The exception, of course, is when we're emphasising something – so you might say, "Can I have a pen" (schwaised) meaning you want a pen (nothing more) or you might say, "Can I have A pen" (pronounced) to emphasise that you want one pen—not two, one. Importantly, this is a DIFFERENT meaning to the unstressed, schwaised "the" or "a".

The schwa is used in far, far more words than these little ones, though.

The Uhmazing Kuhbab

Take for example the word "amazing".

When we're speaking in full flow, that "A" at the front of the word almost disappears – it's like we're saying, "It's pretty 'mazing". But that's not quite right, because it is there.

It's more like a very soft "uh" sound.

"It's pretty uhmazing".

That soft "uh" sound is the schwa.

Back when I was a student most Thursday nights we'd go the town's rock club for a few drinks and some really loud music. And after a few drinks and dancing like idiots until two in the morning, well, we'd all be hungry. So what does your typical drunk British student do?

That's right.

They stop off at the Kebab shop on the way home.

Now, the place we always stopped off had a big fat spelling mistake in its sign. It happens a lot, right?

I always wonder why, yanno, people don't get these things checked before spending a shit load of money on making them. I see signs all over Japan in English that are misspelt, or simply don't make any sense. Having said that, I expect I'll get a thousand emails from people now pointing out all the typos in this book (if you do find any, let my assistant Kim know – kim@doingenglish.com).

But in a way you can't really blame the shop owners. They were Turkish and spoke, let's just say pretty shit English. And they'd simply spelt their sign how you'd expect the word "kebab" to be spelt. With an A.

k-a-b-a-b.

I mean, that's how most British people pronounce it – "Ka-bab". Ka.

But actually, we spell it with "e". And like so many words in the English language, it ain't pronounced like it's spelt – it's not "kee". Nobody says "kee-bab". But really it doesn't sound like "Ka-bab", either. That "a" sound isn't like the "a" in "car" or "carrot". It's kinda soft. Under-spoken. Almost invisible.

That's right.

It's more like Ku-bab. Ku-bab.

There's a little breath of air and an "uh" sound.

It's the schwa sound.

The vowel—the "E"—changes to the schwa. We write, and we spell with "E", but the schwa is not a letter in the alphabet, remember? The schwa is actually ANY vowel that changes to be an unstressed syllable. So where you hear this "uh" pronunciation, that's the schwa.

It comes from quite deep down in your diaphragm. Below the chest (though that does depend a little on the person). And in that sense it's different from other vowels – the vowels all have a tongue position and shape. Whereas this "uh" doesn't come from your mouth (well, it does... but your mouth is kinda doing nothing; you know what I mean).

6

SKIPIN' SOUNDS FOR FLUENCY

I n the previous chapter, we looked at the schwa sound. This is when a sound gets reduced down to something which *almost* disappears... but not quite.

In this chapter, we're gonna go even further and actually lose the sound completely: that is, we're gonna talk about *elision*.

What Is Elision?

Elision is exactly what I just said: It's when you skip a letter, syllable or even a whole word in pronunciation.

When a native speaker speaks in full-flow we're not exactly speaking very precisely. Quite the opposite in fact. Native speaker speech is pretty messy –

but it's ordered chaos, and there is reason to the rhyme, as it were.

Written English and Spoken English Are Not the Same

Written English is a different thing to spoken English. I'm sure you know this... but REALLY get it into your head.

They ain't the same.

So don't try to make them the same.

This applies to native speakers, as well, of course. It happens a lot – you read something many times, but never actually hear it said. And so you pronounce it as you read it... and then someone sniggers 'cos you got it wrong. For the longest time, I thought the word "taciturn" (meaning silent) was pronounced "ta-KI-turn". It wasn't until someone pointed it out in a Youtube video (one of the few times someone's "he got it wrong!" comments was actually correct.) that I realised it's actually "ta-si-turn". Spelling is misleading (if you want to know why English spelling is so fucked up, ask me in the bar one day 'cos it's a favourite topic of mine). You can't trust it.

Now, a common word I hear people getting wrong is the word "literature". And yeah, again, the spelling is misleading. Because it looks like it should be said "lit-A-rach-ure". But it's not. That "A" sound is skipped completely. We say "lit-rach-ure".

In many London accents, people are quite lazy at the end of words. And they would say the word "something" like "somethin" without a "G". There's no observable "ng" at the end. It's "somethin" – "Look: there's somethin' there."

Another common one is "dunno".

"I dunno." That is, "I don't know."

"I dunno" is natural, not wrong. Other examples like this are "Wanna", "Gonna", "Kinda".

They're natural. But with a slight caveat.

Elision Is Variable

It's wrong to think that all people speak in the same way all the time. This certainly isn't the case. Our voices and the way we speak is extremely dynamic. And we naturally fall into the same speech patterns as people around us. Or into speech patterns that we are used to for that situation. A fairly extreme example of this would be myself – the way I speak when I teach is pretty different to the way I speak to my mates in the pub. Which is different again to the way I speak to my wife (when we speak in English, which admittedly isn't often). The words I use are different, and my accent is different. I slur my speech more, get lazy, skip more stuff and speak in a much less polished way. To the extent that when I've been travelling, especially when I got to Ireland (which I go to every three months for a big meeting) and come back home, my wife has a really hard time understanding me in English (as do my kids).

This doesn't mean my "teacher's" voice is fake – everybody does this, even if you're not aware of it. You talk to your mates in a different way to your boss or a client. The point is, everything depends on context.

If you were going to do a formal speech or performance somewhere you wouldn't skip many sounds. You wouldn't say, "Wanna" or "gonna" when giving a speech at someone's wedding, for example. But in the pub with your mates? Totally different.

This discussion goes kinda deep because now we're getting into the topic of register – which is where you change the formality of your speech depending on the situation and the person you're talking to. Again, all you really need to know here is that in a formal situation you wouldn't skip sounds. But if you want to fit in, let's say, socially, in casual situations and not present yourself as someone, very formal and correct and proper (i.e. like someone who only speaks "textbook English") then you would be using elision. Especially the examples that I gave you to do with London speech if you lived here because that's how the people speak.

Get Good at Spotting Elision

One of the best exercises you can do to get really, really good at this is dictation – that is, listening to audio and then writing out everything you hear, as you hear it. What this does is force your ear to hear every tiny little sound (or lack of sound in the case of elision).

This is really good for the schwa sound, too, of course.

The brain is lazy, you see, and we often don't notice the way people talk. This is the same as the schwa sound, and one of the reasons why the "little words" are so damn difficult to learn even though they're the most frequent words in the English language.

The way to do it is simple.

Get yourself some audio that also has a decent transcript (which you don't look at in the beginning). Listen to the audio, writing everything out as you go. It'll be hard, and very, very tiring. But don't check that transcript yet. Rewind the audio and listen as many times as you have to. FORCE yourself to get it. Then when you're finished (and only then), check your written version against the transcript.

It'll be full of mistakes – but this is a good thing because that's how you learn. Extraordinary English Speakers lessons all start with this (which, if you're a member, you'll already know of course). Generally, the places where people make the most mistakes are schwa sounds ("a" and "the" especially) and also missing sounds (i.e. elision).

Don't think I need to say too much about this as it's a pretty simple exercise. Powerful, though.

7

BECOME A MAESTRO OF YOUR VOICE

I n this chapter and the next, we're going beyond your accent. We're going to look more at how you sound as a whole. Which, after all, is what's really important, right? Sounding Awesome.

You see, as you should have already worked out by now, a particular accent does not equal an awesome voice. You can speak just like the Queen or your favourite celebrity and still sound like shit. Or to put it another way, just because you've learned to sound like a Brit or an Aussie or whatever, doesn't mean you actually sound good. Because it's the whole voice and how you're projecting it that matters.

Ask yourself: *what does your voice say about you?*

Is it saying, "I'm amazing!" or is it saying, "I'm trying hard but really I'm not confident at all..."

Be honest with yourself.

If it's the latter, don't worry. We can fix that.

Speaking a language is a physical activity. It's something you do with your body. It's like playing a musical instrument – ultimately it's something you do well by training yourself to do, over time and with consistent, focused practise.

Well, like a world-class musician, you need to learn to manipulate and use your instrument effectively. And that's what this chapter is all about – learning to conduct your voice like a true maestro.

Is It Really Your Accent?

As I've already talked about this in the first chapter of this book, we're all used to hearing a lot of different accents. And although some accents are harder to understand than others if we're not used to them, it's rare that your accent is actually the problem per se.

Well, discounting racial bias or prejudice – but that's a very different type of problem. And anyway, why would you want to please a racist? People like that simply don't matter.

Think of any famous piece of music by a composer. It doesn't sound the same every time that music is played. If an orchestra plays it, the role of the conductor is to bring his interpretation of the music. In one part, he wants more emphasis on the strings. In another he wants them to be quiet. And doing this he creates a certain sound that is quite unique.

There's a well known Japanese TV drama that's quite old now. It was one of my favourites when I was learning the language and one that I recently rented and re-watched with my kids.

It's called *Nodame Cantabile,* and it's basically about a genius conductor to-be studying music. The university has a well-known orchestra that plays to a very high level of technical skill. But then comes along a crazy, fun-loving conductor from overseas who creates a whole new orchestra – the B Orchestra. He fills it with all the weird and wonderful musicians he finds at the university. Creatives and punks who're not interested in performing perfectly, but who want to express themselves in their own way. The orchestra he creates is pretty shit in terms of skill. They don't play their instruments that well, and they're messy. They don't stand a chance of competing against other, better-established orchestras like the A Orchestra.

So they don't try. Instead, they create a totally different type of sound – they experiment and play with the music and have fun. They turn the whole thing into a performance. One that is expressive, full of emotion and grabs people's attention. The music they play is the same music as the A Orchestra plays – but delivery is completely different.

Well, this is the same when you speak – you need to learn to conduct your voice in a way that grabs people's attention.

Become a Conductor of Your Own Voice

The way you deliver the things you say matters. You'll get a totally different result (meaning an impact on people) depending on how you choose to speak.

See, it's not so much your accent.

It's the way you say it.

I used to work with someone—an English teacher —who speaks English fairly well... but she's hard to talk to (and listen to). She's the kind of person who displays little to no emotion, and her face is always a blank slate. You can't tell what she's thinking. Just when you think she's totally bored and pissed off, she turns around and says how much fun she's having. She speaks with a very small, closed, tight mouth and in a way that is quite lifeless. We'll talk more about this later in this chapter, but the point is, if you speak like this you can make HUGE gains simply by improving the physicality of the way you speak.

Moving the muscles in your mouth and face. Expressing yourself visually as well as verbally. Adding tone and emotion to your speech (we'll talk about this in the next chapter). Projecting your voice.

Imagine you go up to someone and start a conversation.

They reply, but their voice is weak and lacks emotion – how do you feel? Probably that the person is bored and doesn't want to speak to you. It's really hard to have a conversation with someone like this, right?

But what if that's *you*?

Well, if you don't want to talk... fine.

No problem with that.

But if you do want to have a conversation with the person? Well, you don't want to be the person who speaks like that. You wanna be the person that is easy to talk to. Jade says, "the mind and the body and the voice is a mirror" – and I totally agree with this. What a person feels about themselves or about other people or the way things are is reflected in the body and in the way they sound. So the person with an energetic, bright voice tells—shows, even—the world, *"I'm energetic and passionate about life."* This has a very different impact on people.

What you've got to understand is that 'communication' isn't just what we say with our words. Rather, it's the result of <u>EVERYTHING</u> about us. From, yes, the words we use, to the tone we speak with, to the pitch of our voice, the energy we project, our facial expression and right down to our posture and the way we stand or sit. Next time you have a conversation in English, try and step back and listen to and see yourself objectively. Once you've got a feel for what you look and sound like now, pick up your 'conductor's baton' and rearrange the ensemble that is your words and sentences to try and improve it.

Make Your Voice Interesting

Rhythm brings texture to the voice.

Texture as a good thing.

A very, very good thing indeed.

It's like the clothes you wear. Different textures express different styles, and when combined well they amplify the colours and cut of the clothes you wear. An outfit could be a nice colour and well cut... but if every item of clothing is made out of exactly the same fabric with the same texture, well, it's kinda boring, right? But when you combine, say, a silk shirt with a rough knit sweater and a great leather jacket and, say, a pair of jeans the overall effect is much more powerful.

Well, the same is true of an interesting voice. The kind of voice we all love to listen to is a textured voice. It varies. Doesn't sound the same all the time. The speaker uses rhythm in exciting ways to get good effects. They play around with the pace of their speech. Speak fast for excitement. Then slow the pace right down to make an important point. Pause for dramatic effect.

If you completely remove rhythm from your voice you become robotic and boring. And robotic voices are hard to understand and listen to.

If you went to university I bet you've experienced something similar, but when I was an art student we had art history lectures once a week. Well, my university had two lecturers.

A guy whose name I totally can't remember. And a woman whose name I've also forgotten.

The guy—probably in his early 60s—was an amazing speaker. He was really, really good at grabbing people's attention and delivering even the most boring art theory in an engaging, exciting way (he also told a lot of sex jokes, but that's beside the point...). His lectures with full of personality and we always looked forward to them.

But the woman?

Jesus Christ... she was quite the opposite. I can only imagine she must have hated her job because she delivered her lectures with a blank expression and a monotonous, droning voice.

Thing is, it was the same stuff.

But when she talked about it?

It was soooo hard to concentrate, and I'd finish every lecture exhausted and with a headache. It was impossible to be interested in what she was saying because the delivered it in a totally boring way. It's hard to listen to monotonous boring droning voices. You've gotta work really bloody hard to concentrate... which is exhausting.

Well, let me ask you: *who do you wanna be? The guy or the girl?* The answer should be obvious.

A good voice is one that's experimental. Playful. One that uses different ways to express itself moment to moment according to how excited the person is, or what they're talking about. Doesn't matter whether it's a serious topic or a fun one – you need to get good at using your voice as an instrument to best communicate your message.

Speaking with Unreasonable Confidence

When you develop your voice something odd happens.

The way you sound changes (for the better).

But not only that – you will change, too.

When you learn to open up and express yourself in English you'll speak with more energy. Your mouth moves better and your body language communicates more. And this all changes the way you feel. And with that, the way people perceive and treat you changes, too. The end result is a massive amount of confidence with yourself that was never there before – all from changing the way you speak. Remember what I said right back near the beginning of this book? Language plays an important social function. It's part of how we bond and maintain relationships, and it's also part of how we demonstrate our position. Weak voice, weak position. Strong voice, strong position.

I know this is true because it's something I've done myself. I was very shy when I was younger – painfully so. It wasn't really until I came to Japan, learned a second language, started teaching and eventually YouTube (we'll talk more about this shortly) and started speaking in front of people (something I never wanted to do, but kinda just fell into it almost by mistake) that I started to find my voice and my confidence.

If you'd known me 15 years ago, you'd never recognise me now. Because the shy, quiet boy of old has been replaced with a man that walks through life with, if I'm honest, an unreasonable amount of confidence. Far less hair too, but we'll leave that for now.

The point is, the only thing that's really changed is that I learned to express and present myself well. And that created a feedback loop that made me more confident.

I've seen the same thing countless times with clients who I've worked with one-on-one and in the Extraordinary English Speakers programme. Learning to speak powerfully breeds confidence. And confidence feeds back into the power in your voice and makes you come across as a more passionate, interesting person. Not just come across as – makes you more passionate and interesting.

There's an idea in linguistics called "Linguistic determinism" that says we can't think what we can't articulate. There has been a lot of argument and research done on this over the decades, but I believe the idea is true (at least to an extent). I also believe it goes deeper than just the words you use. I believe the way you speak changes the way you think, just like the way you think changes the way you speak.

If you're afraid, that fear will come out in your voice.

But if you start to talk in a fearful way... will that make you afraid? I believe yes, it will. And importantly if you're afraid, but speak in a way that is full of confidence, that too will change the fear you FEEL into actual, real confidence.

Breathing Your Way to Fluency

One more thing before we get into some exercises for getting good at this stuff.

Focus on your breathing.

Most people are very, very shallow breathers. And this affects your voice in important ways. If you breathe in a very shallow way, your voice will lack the roundness and texture that people like to hear in a voice. You're also much more likely to sound like you have a nervous voice.

Some people are constantly anxious when they speak. Especially in a second language. Many people don't notice it, but if you listen carefully to the way some people talk, you can hear the anxiety in their voices. You can hear that they're nervous, and it comes through in the way they breathe.

Slow down.

Relax.

Focus on breathing deeper when you speak.

There's not really too much to say about this, because it's something that once you notice, you'll get good at fixing. The problem is that most people don't realise they're doing it—breathing in a very shallow way—because they're so used to it.

Just pay attention to your breathing.

Make it deep.

Breath into your stomach and try to remove all the tightness from your chest and lungs.

Exercises for Becoming a Better Maestro

The good news is that getting good at this stuff is fairly simple.

The bad news is that it's going to take time and experimentation. And a willingness to screw up a bit... or as a lot. Don't worry, though: as I talked about in my book *Magnetic Chit-Chat*, that's fine. There's something very attractive and charismatic about people who are comfortable with messing up. So mess up.

What you want to do is see and hear yourself when you are speaking. This can be literally by recording yourself and studying it, or it can by trying to see and hear yourself in conversation objectively. The 'computer program' running in your brain, like we talked about in Chapter 4. Monitor yourself as you speak, and try and spot the areas that need improving.

Most of us aren't really aware of how we sound when we speak our first language. And we only become aware of the way we sound in our SECOND because we're terrified of making mistakes or speaking it "wrong". And so, we often assume we're good speakers in our first language. But are you really as expressive in your first language as you think you are? Do you look and sound the way you think you do in your first language?

You are your best learning material when it comes to improving this stuff. So study yourself. And I mean noticing and becoming aware of the good parts, too. Not just the bad parts. What are the things about the way you speak that you like? That are impactful for other people in a good way? Do you do these in English, too?

Now, let's look at some more specific exercises for doing this.

Exercise 1

The first exercise I'm going to talk about is shadowing, and this is the most simple, basic of the three.

Shadowing is a great way to work on your overall rhyme and intonation.

I didn't invent shadowing – originally it was (and still is) a test used in speech research to measure fluency. A guy called Alexander Arguelles was, as far as I know, the first person to talk about Shadowing for language learning. And I was the first person to take that and talk about it on YouTube in relation to English learning.

That video went viral around 2008 until I was stupid enough to accidentally delete my whole YouTube channel. I then remade the video in, I think, about 2012.

I'll add the shadowing video I did as a demonstration in the resource area that comes with this book. If you're an Extraordinary English Speakers member, you should be doing this anyway because it's one of the exercises we use. The key word here is "one of", though, because shadowing alone isn't going to do much. There's a lot of misunderstanding out there about shadowing. The video I did has been copied countless times by several different people and blown out of proportion (some people even say it's a method – which it's not). What shadowing is good for is attuning your mouth, tongue, lips and facial muscles to the rhythm and pace of English. So what I like to call the "physical" aspect of fluency. That's about it, though.

The idea is to simply take an audio and speak along with it. Mimic the speaker as closely as you can. Pay close attention to the pauses and the way the speaker chunks their language, blending sounds together as they go. Pay close attention to the speed, and the way the speaker slows down and speeds up. Try and match your own voice as closely as possible. Try and notice the schwa sounds, as well as "missing" sounds.

Again, I'll put a video demonstrating this in the resource area.

Exercise 2

Jade advises you to start with a mirror.

And this sounds like a damn good idea to me too.

Don't worry about what your hair looks like or whether you've done your make up. Instead, take a sentence or a phrase or whatever it is you're learning right now (if you're an EES member take the current weekly lesson and practise one side of the conversation). Practise it in the mirror, paying attention to the way you look as well as the way you sound.

Start by saying it normally.

How do you look? How do you sound? And importantly, how do you feel? Am I saying it with a tiny mouth? Is my facial expression tight or ambiguous? If it is, try and loosen up. Relax.

Once you've got it about right, and you're sounding and looking relaxed, start to experiment.

What if I try and say it with an open expression? Does the sound change? What if I speed up? Slow down? How can I change the effect of what I'm saying?

Play with it.

Try speaking in a very clear, precise way. Emphasise every sound and enunciate well. Now relax and try saying the same thing in a slurred, unclear way. Let all the sounds blend together.

Again, play with it and experiment.

Try and be interesting.

Amy Walker advises people to become comfortable with being weird – well, now is a great chance to practise this. And the weirder you get, the better.

Practise saying whatever it is you're practising in

an over-dramatic way. Be strange. Be weird. Try and make yourself laugh.

Cry your way through a happy sentence. Scream and get angry while saying things that should be said calmly. Deliver your rage with a sweet smile.

And remember: pay attention to your breathing.

Purposely take shallow breaths, to see what it does to your speaking. Then breathe deeply and slowly – how does this change the way you sound and look?

You're trying to build awareness of the full range of your voice. Learning how to manipulate your words and sentences in interesting or impactful ways. And of course, manipulating your facial expression and body language to it further emphasises the quality of your sound.

We'll come back to this in the next chapter, but really there's no right way to do this – it's all about playing.

So PLAY.

Exercise 3

I want to end this chapter with something for the brave.

This is not really an exercise. Not as such, anyway.

But it is an excellent way to improve yourself as a speaker (in your native language too, not just English).

Start a YouTube channel and vlog regularly.

Of course, if your goal is to improve your English, it'd be a good idea to do it in English.

Again, this goes well beyond the scope of this book and just improving your accent and voice. But it is a powerful way to do it. In the beginning, it's a good idea to take other people's videos and "remake them" in your own way (don't copy them; that's plagiarism). For example, on my Japanese vlog channel when I first started it, I did a video saying "happy birthday" to myself. I started by looking at videos other (Japanese) YouTubers had made that were similar and borrowed sentences. Again, this goes beyond the scope of this book. If you haven't read my book "Master English FAST", where discuss a much more complete method for mastering English, then you should check that out and apply what I teach. If enough people are interested, I may do a book about using YouTube as a tool for improving English, too (let me know if you are interested).

The point is though, making videos forces you to look at yourself objectively. When you watch (or edit) your own videos, you spot all the things you are and aren't happy with. Naturally, over time you start to iron out these kinks and speak better and better. Also, because it's public, you've got a lot of motivation (and pressure) to try and improve your videos.

I found YouTube had a very big impact on my speaking overall, and I know Jade has told me the same.

8

CONTROLLING THE FEELING IN YOUR VOICE

I n this final chapter, I'm going to talk about tone and emotion in the voice. Really, this continues on from the previous chapter and could have been included in it. Indeed, we've already talked about a lot of the stuff related to this – but I wanted to separate this out and reiterate the points. This is quite an important topic, and something many people struggle with.

Simply put, tone is the feeling that you put into the things you say – and this can totally alter the meaning of things you are saying. And it can alter the way people perceive you, as a person.

The British Stiff Upper Lip

Culture is a big factor when it comes to displaying emotion in our voices. A good example of this is the traditional idea of the British "stiff upper lip". English people are quite reserved, quite proper, and traditionally at least it was considered better not to show emotion in your voice or body language. When something awful happens, we're not expected to show emotion.

This is the idea of the stiff upper lip.

Don't show emotion.

Don't cry.

Stay calm and carry on.

Britain still retains this to an extent, but perhaps less so than previously. This said, back in 2011 when the big earthquake hit in Japan, I was at the school where I worked. The whole school evacuated to the playground and several students commented, *"Wow, Julian's so calm!"*. I didn't really think about it at the time, but it's not that I was calm, as such. Rather, this is how I felt I had to behave – don't panic, don't show what I'm feeling. Keep calm… and carry on.

This is a silly example, but illustrative: many years ago a friend of mine said that if she got stabbed on the street, first and foremost she'd be embarrassed.

Everybody would look at her with worry in their eyes, and she'd have to admit she was hurt and needed help. This might seem silly to you, but I *get it*. It's a part of our culture not to impose upon others.

The point is, just be aware that cultures approach emotion and showing how you feel differently. It's not that British people don't show emotion in their voice and their tone – it just might be more subtle than something from a culture that lets everything out. I have friends here in Tokyo from Libya, and I'm almost amazed at the sheer power they display in their emotions. When they're happy, they're SO HAPPY. When they're sad, it's like the world is coming to an end.

In my experience, people from Asian cultures often have the most trouble with this. It may be because their language uses tone differently (Chinese for example – which is a slightly different problem, admittedly), or because the way they choose to display tone is different (Japanese culture is similar to British culture, for example). But if you're not careful, the result can be that they don't come across as interesting, engaging speakers. They don't move people with their messages or the things they want to communicate because they're not showing all these things. Which of course, can be a huge limitation.

Lovely Weather We're Having!

Tone totally changes the meaning of things you say. This can be tricky for people learning English as a second language. Well, actually it can be tricky for native speakers too. But, for example, Japanese speakers use tone in a very different way to English speakers. Then the way, for example, Chinese, uses tone is completely different again. In Chinese, the tone you use changes the meaning of a word to another, totally unrelated word. Well, in English tone changes the meaning of complete sentences (though the way it happens is nothing like Chinese of course... so it's a bad analogy). This is especially true in British English, which tends to use a lot of sarcasm and irony. If we say a word with a different tone, the whole meaning of the sentence changes. So even though the words are exactly the same, we shift our tone, and suddenly we have a completely different meaning.

For example, I say, *"Lovely weather today"* – does it mean it's lovely weather? Or does it mean it's horrible weather?

Well, that'd depend on how I say it.

If you've taken my *British Stories* course, you'll have heard me talk about when I was first living in Japan and learning the language. I had a bit of an embarrassing mishap. It was a horrible day, pouring down with rain. And when I arrived at the school where I was working, there was another teacher—a young, and I'll admit, fairly attractive female teacher. And as I walked in, I said (in Japanese), *"Lovely weather today!"*—I said it like a Brit would, in English. It should have been obvious that I meant *"what a horrible day"* from my facial expression and the context. Only it wasn't, of course. Because Japanese doesn't use this kind of ironic backwards-meaning language like British English does. She looked at me like I was a complete moron and turned around to speak to someone else, leaving me feeling foolish.

The point is, it's the tone that's important here, combined with my facial expression and the context.

The words said, *"lovely weather"*.

My tone and body language said, *"what a shit day."*

In the UK at least, it's considered a sign of high emotional intelligence to be able to use and understand this kind of language. Though again, it is something we do more in Britain than, say, the US (which is not to say people in the US don't use sarcasm; they do. It's just not the same).

You've got to be careful, though, when trying to copy this yourself. It's easy to create misunderstandings. I've seen comments on my YouTube videos angry about something I said. But from the comment, it's clear that the person didn't get the joke (and if you don't get this kind of language usage, no, you wouldn't).

This isn't something that can be explained well in a book. But listen carefully to the way people speak in English, and pay attention to their tone combined with their body language. This is yet another reason why you need to let go of individual words and focus on complete phrases, expressions and chunks of English by the way. If you're only listening to the individual words you'll only get the literal meaning. Which as we've just discussed, often isn't what's meant at all.

Also this is, admittedly, much easier for some people than others depending on your cultural background. In my experience, Japanese people tend to struggle with this in English. Whereas people from, say, Poland don't (because it's a part of their own culture too).

The point is to be aware of this kind of communication.

Remember what I said? Everything starts with noticing and awareness. Again, pay attention to the tone that people use. Notice it like you would any other sound of an accent (like we talked about in

Chapter 4) and practise speaking like this yourself (like we talked about in Chapter 7).

Monotone

Speaking in monotone is a problem many people have. If you speak in Monotone you don't convey feeling in the voice. As ironic as this sounds, my secondary school drama teacher spoke in monotone by default. And like the Art History lecturer I talked about in Chapter 7, she was really boring (and tiring) to listen to. Again, ironic, I know. She was a drama teacher.

Whether you're excited, bored or interested and engaged in something... your voice sounds pretty much the same all the time if you speak in monotone. It doesn't change. This can make you sound flat, or, depending on the default tone even irritating to listen to.

Most people who speak in monotone tend to sound quite flat and without emotion. It's very robotic (like we talked about in Chapter 7). But monotone can go the other way, too. Some people actually have a monotone voice that is always energetic, for example. The problem with this is, often they believe that it's best to ALWAYS be positive and happy and don't realise they <u>lack</u> expression because of it. It's not that they come across as bored or uninterested (as my drama teacher did) but rather the opposite – the come across as always happy and enthusiastic. Even when it doesn't make sense. This might happen when someone has grown up in a household where they weren't allowed to not be happy – so they got into the habit of always showing everything how happy and pleased they are, probably because of their parents' emotional problems. But again, this manner of speaking is also problematic, because it lacks the range of tone and emotion that we expect – just like with people who speak in a robotic, emotionless way. Some situations call for being down and depressed, after all.

How to Improve Tonal Quality

So, what's a good way to improve your tonal quality? Really, what we're gonna talk about here is just the same as what we talked about in Chapter 7. And indeed, everything I talked about there applies here, too. This said, I'm going to take the idea of experimenting and building awareness via mirror work a bit further (which is why I'm doing this as a separate chapter). As before, this is something I learned from Jade Joddle, so full credit goes to her for this.

A good way for you to develop emotions and tone is by practising with poetry. Different poems convey different kinds of feelings. You can make a poem about anything, and they come in all kinds of moods, emotions and tones (they're not all about love or clouds or daffodils). Using poetry is a great way to experiment and play around because it gives you a chance to play around with your voice to try to see what happens when you read in different ways.

This is more like a performance than what we did in Chapter 7 – imagine yourself as an actor. If you were standing on stage, acting in a scene, how would you say those words?

What poem you use doesn't matter.

All you're going to do is practise reading it in different ways, just we talked about in Chapter 7. But with a slight difference.

So... take a poem.

Read it.

Now, ask yourself – what feelings do I get from this?

Start with your own interpretation. There's no correct answer here – just go with your own feelings. This is, of course, one of the reasons why poems are so good. They're often quite subjective, and different people will interpret them in different ways. For example, read this line from T. S. Eliot's poem, The Waste Land:

"A crowd flowed over London Bridge. I had not thought death had undone so many."
— T.S. Eliot, Wasteland

What kind of feeling do you get from this? A positive happy one? Unlikely (or at least not from the second part – though you might from the first).

London Bridge is the bridge that goes into the financial district in the city of London where all the money is made. So this line is about what happens in the mornings or in the evenings when everybody flows over the bridge to go to work or to go home. All the wage slaves in their office clothes just going to make money. Hating their work, hating their lives. Pretty heavy stuff (and likely quite relatable).

For now, just focus on this single line.

Read it out loud.

Focus on the gravity of the words. Make your voice heavy, serious. Grave. Dark. Feel the pain of dragging yourself to work on a Monday morning to do a job you hate.

There's no right way to do this; it's all subjective. But remember that a good speech performance is one where you convey the most feeling put the most expression in it.

Go totally over the top.

Nobody else has to see or hear you doing this, so practise to extremes. I want to FEEL the pain and despair in your voice.

Don't get hung up on not being able to say a full sentence without making a mistake. You might make pronunciation errors – don't worry about it. That's not the point of this exercise. The point is to convey as much meaning as you can only using your tone. Elliot's Waste Land is a sad poem – so the way you read it wouldn't be energetic and full of happiness, because that's not likely the emotion you want to communicate. Well, wouldn't normally be, anyway. Because the next step is to PURPOSELY change it in weird ways.

Now, just like we did in the exercises in Chapter 7, we're just trying to build an awareness of how your tone and voice affect the words and changes the meaning.

Fill it with anger.

Hate.

Change the meaning by changing nothing but your voice – read it in an excited, energetic tone.

Make it happy.

Pleasant.

Experiment.

If you already have poems that you like, great. If not, go online and find some. Look up videos of people reading poems on YouTube, and study the way they deliver the poem. And especially the way they use their voice and tone to express emotion. Model them and try and capture the same mood. Or do it in your own way.

To be an effective speaker, it's very important to build a good range of different tones. Become a master of tone. Know how to speak to communicate exactly what you want to say through your tone. As we talked about before, the tone you speak with says a lot about you and is an important part of the messages you want to communicate. It's a big mistake to think you just have to sound happy and cheerful all the time – that's just fake. But it's also a big mistake to speak with no tone at all (or rather in a monotone).

You need to be able to pick and choose the best tone for the situation. This goes back to what we have been talking about all the way through this book. It's all about building awareness. Becoming aware of how people use tone and how people express emotion in their voices. And becoming aware of how YOU use tone and how YOU express emotion in your voice. Then it's about experimenting and playing around with English to what you can do.

Okay.

So I think we've covered about everything here.

Before we wind up this chapter though, let me make one more point: Keep it enjoyable. Try and make this practice something fun that isn't a chore. You might think, *"I don't like poetry."* Well, try and find something that you do like. And if you find one poet that you like, stick with that poet. You could also use song lyrics, though the problem with that is that you already have the song in your head (which bias your interpretation). But again, the key to keep it fun. Play, experiment and learn.

AFTERWORD

With that, we come to the end of Awesome Accent.

Thank you for investing in the book, and thank you for choosing to take your journey to speaking amazing, extraordinary English, with me.

We've covered a lot in this book.

An enormous amount of content, in fact.

The question now, of course, is what are you going to do with the information you've just read?

It's a sad fact that most people will read this book and then never do anything. From the moment I started teaching, I've been frustrated and disappointed again and again. It's frustrating for me personally, because writing this book was bloody hard work–just like producing courses and programmes like EES is super hard work. Sure, it's nice to get your money in my bank account. Ultimately, the sales that come from this book, the courses I make, as well as fees from coaching clients, are what put food on my table, clothes on my kids and beer in my fridge. The money helps me live – this is what I do; my business. But more than that, you know what drives me? My Why? Hearing success stories from people just like you. Hearing that people have applied and implemented my teachings and improved their lives.

Yes, I've heard many over the years. But you know what? I want to hear more.

Do me a favour: do the damn work. Implement what you've learned in this book, do something amazing, and let me know.

Cheers,

Dr Julian Northbrook

SOME FREE RESOURCES

Here are some free resources to further help you on your journey to English mastery.

The Awesome Accent Audiobook

To get the audiobook via the Doing English Learnistic app, simply go this URL:

https://doeng.co/udeQ

Follow the instructions carefully.

If it is your first time accessing the Doing English App, you'll need to install it first (note: this app isn't available in any of the app stores – you need to use the link above). If you already have the app, the book will simply be added to your existing account.

Important: this audiobook is only available via the app, and you need a smartphone that's not older than my grandfather. If you don't have a smartphone and can't use the app, this is unavailable to you.

Doing English Daily Newsletter

I write daily English tips emails, that you can subscribe to for free. Every day at around 8am Ireland time, a new email will hit your inbox packed with tips and ideas for speaking better English. This is also the best way to keep up to date with my new books and coaching courses – which I promote in every email.

Sign up here:

https://doingenglish.com/

The Rocket Launch Method Training

For a summary of the key points from this book in video-format (which lets me visualise some things we talked about here).

Go to:

https://doingenglish.com/freetraining

The Good Shadowing Guide

Shadowing is a great exercise for developing your rhythm, intonation and "chunking" skills when speaking English – but the way most people do it is wrong. This guide will show you how to use shadowing properly and make it work for you personally.

You can get it here:

https://doingenglish.com/shadowing

THE IMPLEMENTATION COURSE

After I originally published this book in 2016, many people said they wanted more: to go deeper into some topics we discuss, and to get my personal help to customise what they've learned here in this book. That's why I created the "Master English *FAST* Accelerator" coaching course.

You don't need this course to implement what you've learned here.

But if you want to see the fastest results, and transform your English speaking in as little as 90 days, it may be for you. I've copied the "basic" information page from https://doingenglish.com/mefa below:

————

Here you can get the basic information quickly, and then if you think the course is right for you... join my free daily emails, and I'll give you the opportunity to get more information and then enrol

What is MEFA?

MEFA is a 12-week group coaching course with weekly study and homework tasks designed to:

- Give you as big a boost in English-speaking proficiency, as possible over the 90-days.
- Get you totally clear about everything you need to do to keep improving with English in your real-life consistently and forever.

Each week's training session, homework task and the daily feedback from Julian is packed with actionable techniques to change the most important parts of your English as fast as possible. The weekly group coaching calls and support you get via the discussion group is designed to help you customise what you learn to you personally.

Requirements

To be right for MEFA, you must meet the following requirements (if you don't meet all of these, there's no point in joining, or even in me sending you more information).

- You must be thick-skinned (I can't work with people who get offended at the slightest criticism).
- You must be able to listen to advice without letting your own (incorrect) opinions about learning English get in the way.
- You must have a real need for English (whether you use English now in work, daily life or have a clear future need – i.e., this is not for hobbyists).
- You must commit to finishing the course. Statistics show the average completion rate for online courses only between 5% and 15%... the completion rate for MEFA is currently 90%. Why? Because I'm extremely strict about requiring you to submit homework, on time, before the deadline. And if you fail to do the work

(and don't have a good reason such as an emergency) I will not hide my displeasure.

Also, one more thing:

The MEFA course is not a magic pill that will transform your English simply by joining and doing nothing.

It takes time and work.

For the opportunity to join and more detailed information about everything we do in MEFA, first subscribe to my daily emails:

https://doingenglish.com/emails

OTHER BOOKS BY JULIAN

These books (apart from the ones which haven't been released yet) are all abatable on Amazon as Kindle and paperback books: https://author.to/JulianNorthbrook

English Learning Books

- Master English *FAST*
- Think English, Speak English
- Fearless Fluency
- Magnetic Chit-Chat
- Advanced English Conversation

For Non-native English Teachers

- The Extraordinary English Teacher [coming soon]
- English Teaching Sales Machine [coming soon]

Vowel diacritic e 51

7

Printed in Great Britain
by Amazon